Camping Adventures With Lora

The Spooky Stories Told Down Long
Winding River

By: Carol Milligan Babson

I dedicate this book to my parents.

Table of Contents

Creature

CAMPING ADVENTURES WITH LORA

The Spooky Stories Told Down Long Winding River

By: Carol Milligan Babson

Chapter 1

The Promise of a Camping Trip

Anticipation has been building up like a balloon overfilled with air that could pop at any time. Ever since my parents started discussing plans for a summer break camping trip down Long Winding River.

I still recall the thrill I felt laying close by the camp fire all snuggled up in my sleeping bag, surveying those beautiful stars above. I remember thinking to myself what a fantastic universe this is.

Three weeks has gone by since summer break began. My friends and I are extremely bored, with nothing much to do. We continue to rehearse what happened at school last year, now...you can imagine just how bored we really are. So I finally get the gumption up to ask my parents, "Whatever happened to the plans for this family to go on a camping trip?"

Don't get me wrong, I absolutely love the country life, but everyone needs a little recreation every now and then.

The closest's town is approximately twelve miles away. There is a movie theater, ice-cream shop, skating rink, and a variety of other stores. The hole in the bucket is this: I'm just not quite old enough to get my driver's licenses yet, so this creates a problem.

Sitting around our dining room table while we eat seems to be where we discuss most family issues.

Today, my parents spring the good news on me that it's possible...for us to go camping this weekend. I guess my question to them last night got the wheels turning. I was even given the go-ahead to invite several of my friends to join us. As you can imagine, this news makes me squeal with excitement. Dad said wait a minute now, "I hate to pop your balloon, but there's one glitch. This trip is on the provision that you...and your friends, if they want to go...assist your mom in getting the family chores done by Thursday night."

I snicker as I say, "If my friends can go we will have a blast!" "Where in the world did you get that word blast from," mom asked? I know, I must have picked it up from dad. Because, I remember hearing him say something like this, "That was a blast from the past," as I let out a huge giggle. Dad also remembered, because he let out a belly laugh and said, "That's my girl."

Just as soon as I finish helping mom wash up these dishes, I'm going to call my friends and invite them.

I just hung up the phone after talking with each of my three best friends. I made them aware of the chores we have to complete if they want to go. I really don't think they mind helping because I could hear the tone of excitement in their voices.

Now, I just have to wait and see if they get permission from their parents.

Plans sure can change quickly, word spread like wildfire about this upcoming camping trip. It now seems there is going to be a total of nine people going. Doug and Kyle are two of my uncles, they are my father's brothers as well as Seth, our friend and neighbor decided to go.

My friends got permission from their parents, and we are all thrilled. My friend's names are Greg, Beth, and Sonya. Greg just turned sixteen, he has his learners permit but shortly he will be taking the test for his driver's license. Just between you and me, I have a crush on him. Beth and Sonya are also fifteen. The three of us girls are excited about taking drivers education when school reopens in a couple of months.

I decide to hit the sheets early tonight, so I set my alarm clock and I slide the volume setting to loud. My friends and I made plans to meet here by eight in the morning, in hopes of completing those "balloon popping" chores.

The alarm rings and I almost jump off of the bed, it startled me so bad that I slapped that clock so hard it turned over on the nightstand. I smell the aroma of bacon and eggs cooking, which makes my stomach growl with a hungry vengeance. So, I wipe my eyes with the back of my hands to remove the sleepiness from my eyes, then I stretch my arms. I recall that my friends will be here shortly to help with the chores. Therefore, I rush to get my morning routine done and then I head downstairs.

I lean over to kiss mom on the cheek and say, "Hey, it looks like you have cooked enough food for a feast." Mom smiles and says, "Set the table sweetheart, I cooked enough for your friends to eat with us. You know we can't work on an empty stomach." Each of my friends arrives one by one and join us at the table.

Mom takes out a paper from her apron pocket, she has written a small list of things to be done on it. The house has to be cleaned, the yard mowed, and the car needs washing. These are the chores that we normally do on Saturdays, but since we will be gone we need to get them done ASAP. Mom decides to start house cleaning.   Greg and Beth made the decision that they want to mow the lawn so Sonya and I will wash the car.

After my friends complete their portion of the chores, they decide to go home and get prepared for the trip.

I walk back to the house and go upstairs. As I walk past the door of my parent's bedroom, I see mom packing up some winter clothes, they have not yet been stored away. I ask if she needs some help, she smiles and says, "Always?"

Before long my stomach starts growling again, oh well, I am a growing girl. After we finish that job, we make a sandwich and some ice tea.

I turn the television on and we sit down to relax for a while. We start watching a movie that just come on, but after thirty minutes mom gets up and walks back into the kitchen. I hear her as she opens and closes the cabinet doors. After the movie goes off, I get up to see if she needs any help. I discover that she has already taken out some food and a few cooking utensils, she has them boxed up to take with us. I'm lucky to have such a wonderful family.

My friends and I are eagerly awaiting tomorrow to get here, because just as soon as my dad, my two uncles, and our neighbor get off from work, we will be leaving for this adventure.

Early the next morning, my friends arrive at our house with some extra changing of clothes, their fishing equipment, and life jackets. We eat breakfast and then we start dragging almost everything out from the storage building behind our house that we think might be useful on this trip. The front yard looks as if we are going to have a yard sale, mostly with camping equipment. I see three, four-man tents rolled up, three lanterns, three coolers, cooking pots and other useful items.

Mom is exhausted, so she is going to take a short break. However, my friends and I have plenty of energy, so we go to the kitchen to get the two small boxes of food and supplies that she has boxed up.

Finally, dad pulls up in the driveway, he is eager to get his boat and trailer secured to the family truck.

Doug and Kyle arrive together in Kyle's truck and right behind them, Seth pulls in the driveway with his vehicle. Doug, Kyle, and Seth each have their own fishing gear, as well as what appears...to be some sleeping bags rolled up. Everyone, including mom, assists with loading the equipment and supplies in the boats.

I overhear Seth and Dad as they discuss which location will be best to use for our campsite, they quickly agree on the elite spot. It's highly motivating to watch everyone smile, I see their faces glow with anticipation. Mom and Dad takes one last look around to make sure they have not forgotten anything.

Dad states, "Load up, it is time to go!" All nine of us secure a seat within one of the three vehicles, we are now ready to depart on this journey.

Shortly after each vehicle arrives at the river, the men take turns backing their boats and trailers into the water, where each boat is set afloat.

We are instructed to put our life jackets on and secure a seat in one of the vessels.

After we are seated, the boat motor engines are cranked up, and we begin our travel along the river.

"The sun is beaming down so hot, I am sure we are all gonna get sunburnt," Sonya says.

While the boats make their way down Long Winding River, my eyes gaze about looking at the beauty of nature. I recognize various types of trees with lush green leaves and pine needles. Many of the live oak trees have Spanish moss mingled all about, the moss sways lazily in the breeze.

As the boat that I am riding on rounds the next bend, I spot a wood duck that has a group of ducklings swimming behind her, they scurry along in a hurry minding their own business. Then to my amazement I spot a flock of wild turkeys racing along the river bank, it appears that the noise of the boat motors is scaring them.

Within ten minutes, the speed of the boats slows down as we approach the chosen campsite. Gently the sound of each boat slides up on the ground where the water meets the river bank. The person that operated/steered each boat steps out and anchors it securely. Then carefully everyone else steps out and starts unloading the supplies.

The sky is a brilliant hue of blue with only a few scattered pristine white clouds that appear to float slowly by.

The sun is so hot we can feel its heat radiate...like it's dancing upon our skin. With each breath, the fresh, clean air filling my lungs and I welcome that occasional gentle breeze that helps to cool us ever so slightly.

The trees sound amazingly alive with different species of birds singing in harmony at once. Freedom from the boat overwhelms me as I race up the riverbank with a couple of sleeping bags clenched within my arms. I stop still in my tracks as I glance over to the other side of the river. I spot several squirrels playing and jumping from tree to tree, I laugh in a low tone so as not to disturb them. I can hear the squirrels as they chatter so intensely that it seems as though they are carrying on a conversation with each other. I motion to the others as they walk up behind me so they can see them at play.

As we survey the surrounding area, everyone seems to be pleased with this location. We each work without end until the tents are completely set up and the camping equipment is in a suitable place where it is easily accessible. Behind the campsite is a vast wooded area, now and then we can hear the scrounging around of rabbits, more chattering squirrels, and what probably could be deer.

Doug and Kyle just warned us to be on the alert for creeping and wandering animals.

"Wild animals like bear have been known to invade campsites searching for food, and snakes slither about anywhere they choose," they both say as they snicker and laugh. Their comment makes everyone apprehensive, so we strain our ears to be on the alert for any abnormal sounds. Those sneaky but adorable uncles of mine make me question their motives, I just feel they are up to something. I would not be surprised if they try and scare us tonight, but I prefer not to spoil their fun by ratting on them. Seth reminds everyone how this river is extremely deep, as well as long and winding as the name implies, he also says that several people have been known to drown here.

Mom, my friends and I decide to remain at

the campsite, but Doug, Kyle, Seth and Dad just left to go fishing. "I'm looking forward to having some fresh fish to eat, have any of you ever noticed how fresh fish will sometimes curl when they are dropped into hot cooking oil?" mom says. We reply, "No."

It has now been approximately two hours since the men left. Mosquitoes and bugs are biting us without any mercy. I already have several whelps and red areas on my arms and legs, I look like I might have the chicken pox. Mom asks the four of us Greg, Beth, Sonya and I to gather some wood so she can build a campfire, in hopes of running off the insects. She warns us, "Watch out and be careful, don't get into any poison ivy, oak, or sumac because if you do your camping trip will be ruined!" Each of us searches the woods for fallen trees and limbs. Luck is with us, we locate some old dried oak and hickory wood that quickly breaks up into smaller pieces. We end up with a large stack of timber after it is all taken back to the campsite. Mom hastily builds a campfire, and then she says, "How would you like to roast some marshmallows, I brought a couple of bags along?" "That is a good idea, we need to find some long sticks to roast them on," I say. We search the edge of the woods just behind the campground and we locate several long, but small circumference limbs growing off of smaller trees. These will be just right to slide the marshmallows on. Everyone agrees to eat only one bag so we can save the other one for a sweet snack later. Eagerly we place our marshmallows over the fire to roast. Beth says, "This is fun, thank you so much for bringing them," as she smiles with appreciation. Mom replies, "You are welcome, I thought it would be a nice surprise." The marshmallows are so gooey and delicious, they seem to satisfy everyone's desire for something sweet.

Just at the edge of dark, the men return with the fish they caught. Uncle Doug and Uncle Kyle start cleaning them, and mom peels some potatoes to make fries...yummy, I think to myself. By the time all of the fish are cleaned, the edge of the night is upon us.

The sky is lovely with a few twinkling stars just beginning to show their faces. Lightening bugs zip about here and there catching everyone's attention.
Mom calls us over to where she is beginning to fry the fish so we can see just how they curl when they hit the hot cooking oil in the frying pan. She's right, they did curl up.
The smell of the food cooking over a wood

burning fire makes everyone hungry with anticipation.

It's rather relaxing to watch the sparks from the campfire burn and to listen to the crackling, popping sounds being made. The burning embers appear to dance wild and free. This reminds me of those silver-sparklers that adults sometimes purchase for their children to enjoy especially around holidays.

Dad starts lighting the lanterns that he hung up on several tree limbs, then he informs everyone that it is time to come eat. We stand in a circle holding hands, as Dad says grace.

The nine of us manage to find somewhere to sit after we fix our plate of food.

The adults mostly talk about their jobs and community events. While my friends and I have huddled closer together, we are telling knock-knock jokes and every once in a while we bring up some funny occurrence that took place at our school in the past. This trip is the most exciting thing we have done since summer vacation begun.   We laugh and giggle so hard that it is difficult to chew and swallow our food without getting strangled. Gregg said,"I think we all have the silly giggles."

Mom and Dad keep glancing at our group and all of a sudden we hear dad say, "What's going on over there with that infectious state of giggling?"   His comment just makes us laugh more.   I whisper to my friends, "The reason we are so happy, is that we are in an entirely different atmosphere and we get to be here together."

The adults are now discussing how the food cooked over the hickory log fire gives it a more pleasing flavorful taste and smell.

My friends and I gathered both oak and hickory wood, but mom chose the hickory wood to cook with. Knowing this I just have to say, "Dad, mom decided to use the hickory wood to cook with, she sure is a smart isn't she?"   Dad responds quickly, "That's the reason I married her as he winks and smiles."

   Most everyone begins to lean backward, as they speak of how full their stomachs are. Dad exclaims, "There's no reason for anyone here to go hungry!"   Everyone nods their heads in agreement, we are all too full to speak.

   Mom asks me to put the used paper plates and any remaining scraps of food we have left in a trash bag. She states, "If we bag our trash and scraps, that will help prevent wandering animals from entering our campsite looking for food." When I finished that task, I joined my friends once again.

Dad and Seth take turns keeping the fire burning so the insects will not bite us.

After a few minutes of silence, Uncle Doug speaks up and says, "I have an idea, I think everyone here should tell everyone else a spooky or an unusual story around the campfire tonight."   "Let's tell the stories in the order of the oldest to the youngest this time, so that means there will be a total of nine stories."   "What does everyone think of this idea?"   Each person agrees and nods their head at the same time.   I think both of my uncles planned this from the get-go so they could have some fun scaring us. There is not a mean bone in their bodies, I love them both, but they do like to have a little mischievous fun.   I guess those two never outgrew that, ha-ha.   "With the moon being full and orange in color tonight, this will be the perfect setting for scary stories," Kyle says with a chuckle as he winks at Doug. Uncle Doug anxiously states, "When everyone is ready, find something to sit on and make a circle around the campfire, and I will start the first story since I am the oldest person here."

I am trying to decide what story I can tell when my turn comes around.

After everyone fixes something to drink, and or goes for an outside bathroom break, all nine of us locate something reasonably comfortable that we can move up close to the campfire to sit on.

"Is everyone ready?" Doug asks. Everyone replies, "Yes." We are eager for the excitement of the stories to begin.

Chapter 2

Uncle Doug's Story-The Ghost of Mr. Mills

Uncle Doug's Story... I remember hearing this story when I was twelve years of age, when some of my friends and I were camping at Hugh's house, he was my best friend and classmate at that time.

It goes like this: Around the date of September 1849 when President Zachary Taylor was president of, The United States of America, the news was buzzing ever where about the California Gold Rush Strike.

This story is based on one particular community that was located in one of the southern states. During the month of October, many family members are busy working in the fields trying to gather their crops. Nonetheless, four fathers from this community decided to pack some of their clothes and buy some mining equipment so they could venture off together to strike it rich. These four men left their families to gather the crops, and so their children could continue to go to school.

In that area, the school was held in the same building that was used as a church and community building for local meetings. In this white-washed structure, there is a wood burning fireplace, four windows, student desks, a teacher's desk, the American Flag, a few basic books, and some writing tablets.

After school is dismissed each evening during the cold months of winter, the teacher and any volunteering students help to gathered wood for the next day. Located behind the school building there is a wooden outhouse, to be used for desperate times.

A man by the name of Mr. Reggie Mills

was the new schoolmaster today because the previous schoolmarm left this town and got married. She left with only a three-day notice, so it took some time to locate and hire a new teacher. Reggie Mills and his wife Vera are new to this community, they are also expecting their first child in approximately three months. There is a total of fourteen students that attends school here, they range from age six to age fifteen.

Thomas is the oldest student that attends this school, and his father is one of the ones that left for California hoping to strike it rich. Thomas had to take on the responsibilities of the farm work and any repairs around the family home since his father left. Some days Thomas would come to school and he would fall asleep on his desk, quite often Thomas had not done any of his homework either.

Thomas tried to explain that his chores at home was taking up most of his time and that he seldom even got a good night's rest. Thomas seemed to be already exhausted most days when he arrived at the school in the mornings.

Mr. Mills tried for a while to be a little more lenient until the school masters life took a turn for the worst. Mr. Mills had been teaching at this school for three full months when tragedy struck, Mr. Mills wife Vera and their child died while she was in childbirth. Mr. Mills felt like he had nothing to live for, his family was gone, he turned bitter and cold-hearted towards everyone and everything.

Two weeks following the death of his wife and child while conducting a class, Mr. Mills asked Thomas, several questions concerning class studies, but Thomas could not answer even one of them. Mr. Mills then asked Thomas for his homework that he was assigned yesterday, but Thomas had nothing to show. The school master's face turned so red it looked as if the blood would pop out of it. Thomas and Mr. Mills were standing face to face and eye to eye. Mr. Mills was so angry that he started yelling that he was going to expel Thomas. This made Thomas so upset that he started screaming back at Mr. Mills as he tried to explain that he had to take care of his family because his father had never returned home from California. The shouting match got so out of hand that before anyone could blink his or her eyes, Mr. Mills had slapped Thomas' face. Thomas was humiliated in front of his peers. Along with the responsibility of having to take care of his family and lack of sleep, Thomas in return slapped Mr. Mills. This sudden impact made the teacher lose his balance and his body fell causing the wooden floor to vibrate. All of a sudden, Mr. Mills grabbed his left arm grimacing, and he gasp for breath, his face was turning purple. Thomas was in a state of shock, his eyes were locked on Mr. Mills as he kept backing away until he could go no further. Thomas' back was up against the wall of the classroom, his face was white as snow, and he looked like he might pass out any second. One of the male students ran out of the school to go find help. The other students in the class stood around Mr. Mills, asking if there was anything they could do to help? The schoolmaster was unable to speak, his face was drenched with perspiration as he took his last breath.

The school remained closed for approximately two months until the community could hire a new teacher. Thomas never returned to school after that day, his family needed his help at home.

This school continued for many years. Teachers and students randomly heard footsteps as the floors would creak and make popping sounds. The plank boards on the floor were old and worn, but everyone thought that Mr. Mills was still walking the floors. The last teacher at this school before it was torn down told how she had seen an apparition in the building several times. The ghost looked like a man wearing dark pants with a white shirt, he had a short full face beard. She told how she could see right through him, and how he could walk right through the wall of the school building. Several adults that were children when Mr. Mills died in that school, described him looking that way exactly.

At present and in the exact location a larger more modern school stands. Students often speak of how the new school is being haunted. At any unknown time, a classroom door may open or close on its own. Books often fall from tables or they sometimes slide right off the shelves of the school library. Many students have said that they feel a presence around them which makes the hair stand on their arms. Often when a teacher or a student walks into a seemly empty room, they have described what sounded to them like they were overhearing two or three people chatting or laughing, for several seconds. One of the voices heard sounds like a very young boy and the other's sound like a female and adult male voice. Even in the gymnasium some people have stated that they have heard what sounds like a basketball bouncing and a child laughing.   COULD THIS BE THE HAUNTING OF THE MILLS FAMILY?   WHERE IN THE SOUTH IS THIS SCHOOL, COULD IT BE YOUR COMMUNITY SCHOOL?

Chapter 3

Seth's Story --Summer Vacation of Terror

I very well remember this family and that summer of terror they experienced. You see, Jake was a close friend and a classmate of mine.

This story consists of a family of five. Frank and Cathy are the parents of Jake age seventeen, James age fourteen and Joan age eleven. At the beginning of the previous year of school, both parents made a bargain with their children. We need each of you to get up when the alarm clock goes off in the morning and get dressed for school without being begged. If you do, we will rent a yacht and take the family on a month long summer vacation, cruising the ocean.

Cathy usually stays at home but on occasion she will assist Frank if he needs her help, since he operates his own business. Frank can leave his assistant in charge if and when he needs to take some time off from work.

"Now that school is finally out for the summer we have to keep our promise," Cathy said to Frank.   Frank did some research on the computer, and he checked out several boat rental business since the family lives only eight miles from the ocean. Each rental market offers brochures to show different designs of the exterior as well as the interior décor of each yacht.   Frank ended up with a multitude of pamphlets that he took home to his family so they could have a say in choosing the most appropriate boat.   Cathy ended up making the final decision based on the interior layout of the kitchen and the sleeping quarters on one particular vessel.

The very next morning Frank went to the bank so he could withdraw some money from their joint savings, he removed what he considered the family would need for a month long vacation. Then Frank drove to the rental office, where he paid a deposit for the yacht Cathy liked, he made them aware of the departure date and he signed an agreement form.

Just as soon as Frank walks in the front door of his home, he is grinning from ear to ear. He said, "Get your clothes packed because we are leaving Friday around noon or just as soon as I get off from work!" Cathy and Frank started laughing as they kept alternating looks between each other and their children, Jake, James, and Joan were happily dancing all around the living room floor.   When their dance of joy was over, each of them ran up the stairs to their bedroom to start packing their clothes and personal items.

Cathy shouted, "Don't forget to pack some rain jackets and other items for those rainy days!"   Cathy takes a seat at the computer where she types a list of things the family will need, including food, fishing gear, clothes and many other essential items.   She takes a few minutes to change her clothes and to let the children know that she is going shopping.   Jake, James, and Joan are so busy packing that they decided not to go with her.   Cathy thinks to herself, we are going to need so much food to stock the kitchen of the yacht, but we will be making numerous stops at different ports along the way.

Friday at noon Frank arrives home with a

lot on his mind. The house has to be secured, I have to pay a few monthly bills, notify the mail service, make sure all appliances are off, and take care of some other necessities. Cathy arrives home, she chats with Frank for a few minutes and then she goes upstairs to make sure their children has their clothes and personal items packed.

Frank pays the most important bills online and then he shuts down the computer. Then Frank makes a phone call to the postal service asking them to hold the family mail until further notice. Frank walks around and surveys the inside of their home as he turns most of their appliances off. He takes care of a few more final loose ends while everyone else is loading the family van with luggage, food, and other supplies. Now that the house is secure, the van packed, and everything else is prepared, they anxiously get seated in the vehicle. As Frank backs the van out of the driveway, Cathy takes one last glance at their home to make sure everything looks in order. Jake, James, and Joan, seem so happy, delight is written all over their faces.

As their vehicle pulls into the entrance of the boat dock, everyone yells with excitement. Cathy says, "Now, I know you are in a hurry to leave, but it is going to take some time to unload the van and pack everything on the boat." Each family member continues to work hard until everything is in its proper place on the rented yacht. We are still not quite ready to leave. Frank turns to walk off of the boat dock, "I have to park and lock the van in the designated area. After that, I have to pick up some final documentation and get the yacht keys at the office."   As Frank walks back up the boat dock, he holds up the yacht keys as they dangle from his fingertips, he says, "We are ready to go." Everyone laughs with joy.

Frank stands near the bow of the yacht operating it as it begins to move forward. Cathy is walking to the kitchen area. Jake, James, and Joan are standing near the stern of the yacht waving goodbye to the rental boat employee. Everyone is happy that the long-awaited vacation has finally begun.

The first two weeks goes exceptionally well. They enjoy fishing, swimming, sunbathing, relaxing and all the joys of life, plus the warm feeling of being a close knit family. With no land in site, Frank tells Cathy that they are now several-hundred-miles from the port where they first left.

The family has caught and ate so many

fishes since their vacation started. When they clean the fish, they typically use a covered gallon bucket to put the fish heads and entrails in, and most times they even put in the scraps that they have left over from their meals. This gallon bucket is almost full, and as Jake opens the lid to add more scraps the fumes overpowered his nostrils, it has the worst putrid smell. Jake lifts the bucket over the rails of the boat on the starboard side and dumps the contents overboard.

Jake goes to the bathroom sink to wash his hands. Then he decides to phone a couple of his friends, Joe, and Seth (that's me). Jake is curious about a girl named Anna that he has a crush on. Anna attends the same school, and he wants to find out what she has been up to so far this summer. Jake also wishes to know if there is anything new going on in the neighborhood. After talking with his friends for nearly forty minutes, Jake asks James if he would like to go swimming since the boat is now anchored.

Frank is now in the sleeping quarters trying to get some much-needed rest and sleep, he has been up steering the yacht ever since yesterday evening, and he is exhausted. Jake thought the contents of the bucket had sunk, and there would be no problem with swimming on the port side of the boat. James agreed, and they both jumped in the water at approximately the same time. Joan is lying on a beach towel sunbathing while listening to her mother's old battery operated transistor radio using a set of earphones. Cathy is in kitchen tidying up, the outside cabin door is closed so no outside noise will wake Frank.

All of a sudden Joan thought she heard a noise even though she was wearing earphones, is that someone screaming she thought to herself as she jumps to her feet? The music from the radio along with the earphones make it difficult to hear outside noises. Joan suddenly jerks out the earphones and she hears terrifying screams. Joan runs to the port side of the boat from where she heard the cries. As she gazes downward into the sea water she screams with every emotion inside her, she cries out for her mom and dad to come quickly. Jake and James both are thrashing about fighting for their life in an enormous pool of blood, both boys scream once more as they are being pulled underwater. Joan runs to get her mom, but Cathy is already on her way to wake up Frank after hearing the screams. Frank is awakened by the cries of help coming from Cathy and Joan. He jumps up from his bed and runs out to the deck. Joan has difficulty speaking full sentences because her tears are mixed with screams, but she is able to get enough words out that it lets Frank know the boys have disappeared underwater.

Frank immediately jumps in and right behind him Joan leaps into the water, they have no thought of safety for themselves. Frank is yelling over and over in a panic, "Jake, James where are you?"

All of a sudden Joan screams out in terror and pain. Frank turns to look for Joan and he sees her right hand as it disappears in a massive pool of blood. Frank is frantic as he tries to swim to the site where Joan was so he can dive down to rescue her, but he is never able to swim that far. Something caught Frank's mid left lower leg and foot completely severing it.   Cathy is on the deck screaming out in panic and shock pleading for Frank to get back on the yacht.

Frank is exhausted, but he manages to reach the boat ladder.   Cathy hysterically reaches down and grabs his left hand pulling him with all the strength her body can withstand.   Frank falls onto the boat-deck, he is unable to walk and he is bleeding profusely.   Cathy now sees the ocean water around the yacht swarming with Great White, Tiger and Bull Sharks hungry for more. Frank's mid lower left leg is gushing bright red blood.   Cathy instructs Frank to take his hands and hold pressure, until she can take his belt off and cord his leg.   All the while they are screaming and crying out for the loss of their children.   Frank's face is as white as cotton, and he starts gasping for breath.   Within a couple of minutes, Frank passes out from blood loss.

Cathy is in a semi state of shock but just as soon as she can think of what to do next, she makes her way to the mobile radio unit. Cathy has difficulty operating the system, but finally she is able to contact the Coast Guard. Within fifteen minutes, a helicopter is hovering over the yacht, and a basket is being lowered with two Coast Guard men in it. The two men lift Frank's body and they place him in the basket, he is then elevated into the helicopter. Next they assist Cathy and when she is seated in the chopper, she observes a medic starting an IV in Frank's right arm. As they are making their way to the nearest hospital, Frank began to revive. The Coast Guard medic told Frank and Cathy that one of the Coast Guard members stayed on board the yacht, and he would take it back to the port from where it had been rented.

When Frank arrives at the hospital, they give him blood. Then he is taken to surgery for repair at the amputation site. Frank now wears a prosthetic left lower leg and foot.

"Our lives were turned upside down that year. We will always have our family memories, and the love we have for Jake, James and Joan will never be forgotten or replaced," They said.

Frank and Cathy have now adopted two children, they are real brother and sister. At the time of adoption, Timmy was three years old, and Lauren was two. Frank said, "We will always continue to take vacations, but for this family safety will be first and foremost."

Chapter 4

Kurt's Story--The Uneventful Hunting Trip

I remember camping in this exact spot when I was approximately nine years old, that's the reason I chose this place. The campsite looks much like it did that night long ago. When my father, three of my friends and myself were camping here. I am telling this story as my dad told us that night approximately forty-one years ago.

This story occurred sometime around 1937 in one of the Southern States of America. It was during the season of late fall and many of the trees had already shed their orange, yellow and green leaves.

Three men by the names of Tom, Blake, and Henry were concerned about their family's food supply because winter was fast approaching. These three men and their families lived in the same community and all three of them decided to take the next three to four days to hunt and fish. They made plans to leave early the next morning, so each of them returned home to gather up what supplies they thought they would need.

As expected the men meet at the designated area early the following morning.

Blake had his horse hitched to a mid-size wagon to carry most of their supplies. Each man took a box that contained ice in hopes of packing their game and fish in it. They each brought a couple of homemade quilt for bedding, guns, fishing equipment, some cooking utensils, and a little extra food and coffee to share. They decided to follow an old trail that had been in the woods for many years, and they knew that somewhere down that trail there was a good stream for fishing. Blake walked ahead to led his horse, Tom and Henry followed behind just in case something was to fall off the wagon. The hunters walked that first day until dusk of evening. They were so tired they decided to stop and set up camp. They collected enough firewood for the night and built a campfire. Each man unrolled his quilts to make a bed and placed them where he chose to sleep. It's late, so the men decide to prepare some food they brought from home along with a pot of coffee. After eating they were so tired that they suddenly fell asleep before they cleaned up the campsite of any uneaten leftover food. Earlier they had discussed how they needed to get a good night's rest so they could put in a full day of hunting and fishing the next day.

Approximately three hours after the men had fell asleep they were awakened by the sound of something charging through the woods, it was making a fierce snorting sound. They could also hear the sound of small tree limbs breaking and bushes being trampled. The three of them lay quietly in their beds hoping that they would not be bothered.

Within the next four minutes, two large wild boar hogs with long razor sharp tusks ran straight for Henry. He happened to be lying closest to the uneaten food, the boars hogs could not resist the smell of this delicacy. Henry quickly rolled over onto his stomach and buried his head face down into the ground. He then pulled his cover over the back of his head for protection. The swine jabbed their tusks several times into

Henry's quilt while snorting with intent to find the food.   Once they observed the food, they trampled across the top of Henry's body.   Henry remained as still and quiet as possible.

Tom and Blake grabbed their weapons lying next to them. Tom said, "Take the one on the left."   Within a blink of an eye, Tom and Blake stood up fast and shot both hogs. Henry remained quiet and still until they told him the animals were dead.   Tom and Blake walked over to check on Henry's condition, they saw where the hog's sharp tusks had ripped holes in Henry's cover. Upon examining his body for damage, they saw six small puncher wounds that were bleeding.   The men assisted Henry with wrapping his wounds, they used strips torn from an extra tee shirt that Blake found in the wagon.   Henry is lucky that his major arteries were not punctured, and within a short time the bleeding stops. Henry said, "I guess anything can happen when you least expect it to." Henry helped Tom and Blake as much as he could to clean the hogs, they divided the meat three ways and packed each person's portion in their own ice box.   The men managed to get a couple more hours of sleep that night.

At daylight, they got up feeling tired and unrested. Each one grabbed a quick snack from some of the food they brought from their homes and drank a cup of coffee. They hope to hunt and fish as much as possible today, so they start their venture looking for wild game and any fishing streams they might find.   Henry walked as much as could, but at times he would have to ride in the wagon since his body was sore.

They had an exciting day, they each shot a deer which would provide extra food for their families. After preparing those deer, they still had enough daylight to do some fishing after they located the stream. The fish were biting great that evening, and within a short time they each had a string of them.

The men chose to set up camp close to the stream so they would have plenty of fresh water to use. Once they gathered some wood, they started a campfire. Then they cleaned and cooked the fish. They made sure to bury any leftover food, hoping to have a restful night.

There had not been any rain the past couple of weeks and the ground was dry. The temperature outside felt a little warmer so the men moved their beds further away from the still burning campfire.

They are unaware of any impending danger while sleeping but the campsite is plagued by slithering snakes. The snakes are even crawling over their bedding, and it just so happens that it woke Blake up when one of the snake's tails slid against his face. In fear, Blake alerts Tom and Henry about the snake infestation. Tom slides out from under his quilt bed cautiously, as he stands up he reaches over and picks up a small tree limb that had previously fallen. Tom took one of the extra shirts from the wagon and wrapped it around the end of that tree branch, he then lit the shirt from the campfire to make a burning flame. Tom took the torch and scared the snakes away. Blake makes a comment to us, "I bet the snakes were hunting water since it's so dry in this area. That was scary, I sure hope that never happens to me again." The guys put more logs on the fire hoping the snakes will not return, they end up staying awake drinking coffee the remainder of the night.

Just at daybreak they cook a hearty breakfast, but they often yawn from lack of sleep. Since their campsite is so close to the stream, they decide to do some more fishing. As evening approaches they ended up with an abundance of fish, it takes quite some time for the guys to get them all cleaned. As they pack the fish in their boxes, there is no room for the last remaining nine of them. Tom, Blake and Henry's clothes and hands are slimy, they reek with the scent of fish. The men decide to cook and eat the remaining nine fish that night.

Blake said, "I think we should build a large fire tonight so the snakes will not bother us." With a doubt in his mind, Tom snickers and says, "Nothing else can possibly go wrong tonight...can it?" The three of them look at each other and laugh. "I believe we are all about ready to go home tomorrow," Henry said. The men end up sleeping on top of their quilts because it's so hot with that giant fire burning.

Who would believe it, but at two forty-five in the morning a large black bear entered the campsite? The bear is sniffing the air as he makes a huffing, snorting sound. He turns and walks straight to the wagon where he starts pawing at the boxes containing their venison and fish. All this noise has already woke the guys up. Tom, and Blake each climb a different tree. Henry is too sore to climb, so he checks his gun to make sure it's loaded, with one shot between the eyes that bear hit the ground. Only after Henry makes sure the bear is dead, would Tom and Blake come down from the trees.   It took all three of them to load that humongous bear on the wagon. They decide to start their journey back home, so they put the campfire out and pack up their supplies.

The men go to Henry's home first to skin the bear and they share the meat.   Henry's family is delighted about the new bear-skin-rug they will eventually have.   Each family is thrilled with all the fish, venison and bear meat.   The guys discussed whether or not to tell their loved ones about this adventure....WOULD ANYONE BELIEVE WHAT HAPPENED ON THIS TRIP?

Chapter 5

Uncle Kyle's Story--The Escaped Convict

Steam rising from the asphalt, so hot I believe an egg would almost fry on it. It was late July in the South, and the sun felt like a hot oven baking. Sweat was pouring from the convict's bodies as if they were in a hot steamy sauna. The stink of perspiration was all around the eighteen men that were working to near exhaustion. Using bush axes and sling-blades they slash thru the overgrown weeds that had taken over the sides of the road. Sitting in prison was no picnic but this punishment had to be agony, for those men. They were offered an occasional drink of water to quench their thirst. "You men have to cover a quarter of a mile before we can call it a day, and then

we will head back to the prison yard,"
Prison guard Davis said.   Several of the men
whisper in a low soft tone so the guards
can't hear them, "I don't think I can make it,
It's too hot and I am exhausted."   Both
guards seem to be tired, they keep shifting
their weight from one foot to the other.
Their gun barrels glisten as the sun beams
down on them, but they hold steadfast onto
their rifles.   Prison guards Ron and Davis
turn to face each other as Ron strikes up a
conversation about plans that he and his
family has made for the upcoming
weekend.   Davis even spoke about his
plans to take his family for an overnight stay
near an amusement park.

Daniel, one of the convicts, quietly
stepped over a small ditch that separated
the roadside and the woods.   The guards
continue to talk for a short time never

hearing Daniel as he escaped. The other seventeen prisoners fill in the empty spot where Daniel stood without ever saying a word. Daniel continues to inch away until he is far enough to break and run without being heard, then he runs so hard that he starts gasping for breath. About the same time as Daniel comes up on a river bank, the two guards discover that Daniel is missing. Both guards knew they would be reprimanded for letting Daniel escape. Prison guard Ron radios for backup and the need for trained search dogs. Daniel slid down the bank of the river and he steps into the fresh water to hid his footprints, he runs until he begins to stagger from exhaustion. Daniel stops long enough to lean over and put both of his hands on his knees so he can catch his breath. All of a sudden Daniel stands up quickly straining his ears, thinking he heard something in the distance, he now hears the dreaded sound of dogs barking. Panic fills Daniel's body and he runs for life. The sound of the dogs was beginning to get louder, Daniels mind was racing with the thoughts of: where can I go and what should I do now?   The only solution he could think of was to cross the river and head further into the thick woods.   The only thing stopping Daniel was the knowledge that he had never learned to swim, but he felt this was his only chance. Taking a big deep breath of air he made an attempt to swim across the river.   As Daniel reached halfway, the calves of his legs began cramping.   Daniel is fighting for his life as the water splash's over him, and it fills his lungs. Daniel lost the battle right there.   Daniel's remains have never been located.

One group of five people that were camping down Long Winding River told what they happened to see during one of those days. They described it as an apparition or a transparent figure of a man that appeared to be in his mid-twenties. They saw him running as water splashed around his feet, he was panting and gasping for breath.

Numerous other people whether fishing or

camping have also described seeing what appears to be someone running in a rush near the edge of the river bank, gasping for breath as though they were being chased.

I would advise everyone to be on the

lookout! DANIEL JUST MIGHT VISIT THE NEXT TIME YOU ARE CAMPING OR FISHING IN THE RIVER.

Chapter 6

Micky's Story--TERROR TWO

Oh MY! So many tales have been told regarding these twin girls, everyone called them the TERROR TWO, but I will only reveal a few devious tricks those girls pulled. Approximately twenty-eight years ago I graduated from high school with Sky and Joy. These girls had an attitude of, I am a princess, and you will pay if you upset our world.

Our classmates can remember how Mrs. Miller our fourth-grade teacher was a victim of their harassment just after the third day of school that year. Was it because she gave out homework assignments, or could it have been another reason? I never discovered their reason for sure. The

TERROR TWO arrived at school extra early that morning with an apple and a bottle of clear thick glue. Joy and Sky entered their homeroom and walked straight to Mrs. Miller's chair, and they emptied the entire container of glue in the teacher's seat. The girls quickly closed the classroom door behind them; they were never observed by any staff member or student. Standing near the hall lockers, they waited for the morning bell to ring for class. As the morning school bell rang, Mrs. Miller walked into the classroom with her students and the TERROR TWO TWINS following behind her. Sky and Joy sat the apple down on the teacher's desk, Mrs. Miller was thanking the twins for the Apple and at the same time she was pulling out her chair to set down. The girls took their seats, looking like perfect angelic angels.

Studies continued uninterruptedly for an hour. However, just as soon as Mrs. Miller needed to write some math problems on the blackboard, she could not stand. No matter how hard she tried to free herself from the wooden chair, it would not release her. Mrs. Miller said, "Mary will you go and locate Principal Simms, let him know that I need his assistance as soon as possible." Principal Simms and Mary immediately returned to Mrs. Miller's classroom. Just as quickly as Principal Simms surveyed the situation, he dismissed the students for recess. Principal Simms requested the aid of two other female teachers in the nearby classrooms for help. The two other female teachers tried to pull on Mrs. Miller's dress hoping to free her but it was glued steadfast. Mrs. Miller asked if anyone had any article of clothing that she could use to cover herself with since her dress would have to be cut to release her. Principal Simms offered the use of his extra white shirt that was hanging in his office, he keeps one there just in case his shirt gets soiled. Principal Simms left the room and then promptly returned with his shirt, Mrs. Miller voiced her appreciation. After one of the other teachers had cut away the bottom of the dress Mrs. Miller was wearing, she wrapped the white shirt around her to cover the exposed portion of her body. Mrs. Miller went home long enough to change into another dress, and then she immediately returned to school. Principal Simms replaced Mrs. Miller's chair with one that he located in a classroom that was not being used at this time.

That secret remained silent until the TERROR TWO TWINS bragged several years later about the many things they had done to get revenge.

Who's day can we make rotten today seemed to be the TERROR TWOS attitude? Just like the day the school gym class was running around the track, and Sky tripped on her own two feet. It just so happened that James one of our classmates was the closest person to her, and she accused him of making her fall. Of course, Joy runs to Sky's defense, and they plotted revenge as usual.

In the cafeteria, the boys usually have a designated area where they normally like to sit, so this made the prank easier. The next day just before lunch Sky raised her hand, and she asked her teacher if she could go to the bathroom? When she left out of the classroom, she took her pocketbook with her but instead of going to the toilet she headed for the cafeteria. Sky walks over to where James usually sits in the cafeteria, and she loosened the top on the salt shaker. Sky then exchanged the sugar container from school with one that her family had at home, but instead of sugar this one she had filled with salt. Just about the time Sky got back to her class the bell rang for a lunch break. That day's menu was: meatloaf, mash potatoes, garden peas, chocolate cake for dessert and a choice of milk or tea. After James had his tray of food, he went to his usual seat, and as he went to salt his mash potatoes, the whole shaker emptied into his potatoes. As usual James wanted to add extra sugar to his semi-sweet tea and instead, salt was what he got again. Well, at least James had meatloaf and chocolate cake that was edible. James became very suspicious of the twins because every time he walked by the girls they would giggle.

That following Saturday their parents had made plans to visit some of their out of town friends for a cookout, but the TERROR TWO did not want to go. The twins had decided that on Friday night before the family's scheduled visit with their out of town friends they would prevent this trip. Joy would hide her dad's favorite shoes, and Sky would sneak into their parent's bedroom after they were asleep and take the car keys and hide them. Sky hid the keys down the side of her dad's recliner. The TERROR TWO got their way; the trip was called off. The Twins have also been known to remove money from their dad's billfold if he refused to give them what they wanted.

Just for laughs and with no apparent reason the TERROR TWO had been known to hide the neighbor's newspaper. Once they even locked the neighbor's cat inside the neighbor's brand new car, and the cat clawed those leather seats, ruining them. One Sunday the TERROR TWO should have gone to their age-related class for their Sunday-school lesson. Instead, the girls came out to the parking lot and leaked a tire down from four different vehicles, and one of those was Preacher Ward's car.

They even pulled pranks at various restaurants. Once they took a couple of worms and a dead fly with them to a local eatery, at this self-serve cafeteria, people regularly dip their own portion of food. The TERROR TWO placed the crawling worms and the dead fly on two separate containers of food. Most everyone that was eating at this restaurant that day got up from their table and left, after hearing three ladies scream out in disbelief as they described what they saw.   For a short time, the restaurant had to close their doors, after the incidence.

By the time, they reached the tenth grade of school no one would have anything to do with the TERROR TWO TWINS, not even their classmates. The classmates organized a secret meeting to discuss how to repay them back for all of the stunts the TERROR TWO had pulled on them through school. No one would ask the girls to go on a date, they even went to the prom alone.   At the prom that year the seats were reserved for everyone, with name tags on the banquet table. A couple of guys in our class put blue ink in the seats that the twins were assigned to sit in; to get them back for the stunt they pulled in the fourth grade with Mrs. Miller. The blue ink ruined the twin girl's prom dresses, the whole bottom portion of their gowns where they sat in the chairs looked like a hunters target site stained with ink. The only time they danced at the prom was with each other.

Everyone that had been tortured by the TERROR TWO planned somehow to pay them back that year.

Today the sisters have married and changed their way of life. Joy married a preacher, and Sky married a well-known lawyer. The weirdest and funniest thing is that they both have four children each, and their children are now pulling some of the same devious tricks that the terror two twins pulled. SO I GUESS WHAT GOES AROUND DOES COME AROUND! WELL, EVENTUALLY ONE DAY

Chapter 7

Greg's Story --The Unknown Creature

Located near the mountains there is a beautiful lush green valley with a sparkling stream, it is lined with mountain rocks of various sizes. As the water in the creek flows downward, it splashes against the rocks causing a cold spray of water mist that refreshes the skin of anyone standing close by. There are multiple types of trees everywhere you look, as well as flowers and jasmine vines in full bloom.

Bob, Rick and Gene ages fifteen to eighteen begin setting up a campsite within close view of the water. They made plans to camp the whole weekend, Friday thru Sunday and to return home sometime Sunday night.

The air has that clean just rained fresh smell that is mixed with the scent of jasmine. Now and then the guys spot some mountain trout leaping in the creek, their fish scales, and fins reflect the sun, which makes them glistens with the colors of the rainbow. "That would make a terrific meal," Bob said, with a chuckle. After the camp is set up, and the wood is gathered so a campfire can be started later, they decide to go fishing. Within two hours, the guys have a beautiful string of rainbow trout. Gene proceeds to establish a campfire as Bob and Rick start cleaning the fish. In no time at all the boys are discussing girls and in the next few minutes they are talking about how happy they are to be here camping. After cooking and eating the fish, they each stretch back and enjoy sitting by the fire relaxing.

Gene casually told them what had happened three months earlier, he said that some of his other friends had been scared away from this exact campsite by a creature. Gene said he did not know if it was true or if they were just trying to scare him since they were aware he had made plans to come here this weekend. Until Gene made that comment about the monster, they were all thinking how beautiful the sky was and what a good week for them to be here since no rain was in sight. However, this comment made them have an uneasy feeling that something could be lurking out there that does not want anyone invading their territory. It's now getting late, and they begin to yawn one time after another, finding it difficult to stay awake. They each get comfortable in their sleeping bag and soon the guys are snoring.

Within a couple of hours, they are awakened by two owls hooting back and forth to each other in the distance as if they are sending warning messages. No other unusual sounds were heard until three-twenty in the morning. All of a sudden Bob, Rick, and Gene sat straight up in their sleeping bags, loud heavy stomping sounds awaken them. Their hearts are about to pound out of their chests with fright, the guys are terrified. Bob, Rick, and Gene have an eerie feeling of being watched. The beast is walking so close to the bushes and trees that it has caused the camp site to turn a darker shade of black like an enormous shadow has been cast over the area. Loud grunting sounds are heard as it moves about and every now and then it lets out an ear busting yell so loud that the men have to cover their ears.   It sounds as though the beast might be calling out to its mate.   The creature continues to grunt and stomp its feet until it gets further and further away and can no longer be heard in the distance.

The boys add some logs to the fire, in hopes of scaring off any unwanted creatures.   Bob said, "What do you think that was?"   Rick spoke with a trembling voice, "I sure don't know, but I'm about ready to go home, are you guys?"   "We can decide that later today, it may have just been a giant bear and chances are it will not be back," Gene said.   They chat about the incident for some time, and they finally come to the conclusion, that it did not sound like any bear they had ever heard before.

The boys nodded on and off the rest of

the night, but they remained anxious as they listened for any unusual sounds or movements.

The next morning they still felt tired from lack of sleep. They prepared a few eggs and bacon that they had brought from home for breakfast. After chitchatting they decided to stay close by the campsite today, they were afraid to venture out very far or apart for fear of meeting up with this strange creature.

The guys managed to kill enough birds for their evening meal, but the chore of picking feathers and cleaning the birds was a difficult task. It was the edge of the dark by the time all the birds got prepared. The three boys had now...convinced themselves that maybe it could have been a bear that they heard last night.

They decide to cut their trip short and

make tonight their last night of camping. The birds cooked over the campfire made an excellent meal for them. Just after they finish eating, they gathered some extra firewood, and Rick places a couple of the logs on the fire.

The boys find a comfortable spot near the campfire to rest. Then all of a sudden, they hear a flock of birds' behind the campsite, it sounds as if they took flight in a panic to get away quickly. Next, they hear what sounds like several deer running to escape danger. They are beginning to get an uneasy feeling. The dark of night is upon them. In the distance, the boys believe they are starting to hear the same commotion that they heard last night. The stomping and grunting sounds are getting closer and closer with each step the creature takes. Now all of a sudden, it makes that same ear-piercing scream that bellows out once more. Ever what this creature is just broke through the trees, its eyes are glowing red and vicious. Bob, Rick, and Gene back away until they are standing on the edge of the stream. As the beast like creature turns away, it slaps at the trunk of a small tree breaking it into, just like it might have been a match-stick. All of a sudden it let out another scream, then it stomps off until it can no longer be heard.

Never wanting to come in contact with this creature again.   We quickly put out the fire and gather our hunting equipment, sleeping bags and other camping supplies. It's unknown what type of animal this is, but they knew the experience was real for them.

That night the boys slept peaceably in a motel room, and they returned home the

next day.   Believe it or not, make your decision but this escapade gave them a fear of the unknown.   They will most likely go camping again, but I am confident that they will choose a different location.
WOULDN'T YOU?

Chapter 8

Beth's Story --Spirit of an Indian Maid

I would like to pass on her story to you, as I remember my Great Grandmother telling me when I was the age of six. She passed away to the great beyond just nine months after.

My Great Grandparents enjoyed the simple way of life before and after Grandfather had stopped working, they fished a lot in the river that was within a safe walking distance from their modest home. All that separates the river from their backyard is a large cleared field. The area is generally used for gardens or farming crops, and beyond the field there is a small head of woods.

She said, "Close to the area where the

track joins the edge of the tall trees; there once was a large American Indian Village. Around this area, they were able to feed their families with plentiful game and fish. Indian made pottery and arrowheads have been found in the ground and all around the river bank."

One day Great Grandmother went for a walk, she said she felt the need to get out of the house and enjoy the beauty of that mid-spring day. While she was walking in the field close to her home, she kept seeing a flash of light or beam as if something was being reflected from the sun's rays. She tried to judge the whereabouts of that reflection as she walked up to a large tree stump. At some point in time from the way the stump looked, it appeared that there could have been a hollow hole in that tree. Reaching down into the stump, she grasped onto what felt like a smooth stone. It took her quite some time to get this object released because a string had attached itself to the inner workings of the wood. What she observed was a large beautiful turquoise flat stone. The stone was wrapped in what appeared to be strings of buffalo hide. In my Great Grandmother's imagination, she wondered if it might have been chewed by some young Indian maid to make this soft, thick string. The Buffalo string was uniquely wrapped and woven to hold this turquoise stone, lines hung near the end to tie the necklace around the person's neck. She wondered all the way home about who might have owned and wore such a beautiful object like this.

After arriving home, she gently cleaned the necklace with a soft damp cloth and stretched it out on the table to reshape it back to normal and to let it completely dry. So anxious to wear the necklace she kept feeling it; the stone had an unusual warmth about it. My Great Grandmother said that she knew this might sound crazy, but she sensed the stone was happy to have been found. She lifted the necklace and cautiously tied it around her neck; she went to the mirror and admired this lovely work of handmade art.

When Great Grandfather arrived home that evening, she ran to show him her find. He questioned her about how and where she found such a beautiful object. My Great Grandfather said, "It is beautiful, it matches the color of your gorgeous eyes."

While getting ready for bed that night she loosened the strings and laid the necklace outstretched on a table near their bed.

Closing her eyes and gently taking a

couple of deep relaxing breaths, she soon drifted off to sleep. Her mind envisioned a beautiful spring day, with a fragrance of honeysuckle vines in the air. She viewed members of the Indian Village going about their daily task but what caught her attention most was a gorgeous Indian girl with brown eyes and long brown hair that seems to be unhappy. This Indian maid was wearing a necklace just like my Great Grandmother had found, maybe that is the same necklace. The Indian girl appeared to be in her mid-teen years, and she had been betrothed to the Indian Chief's son at a very early age. However he was not the man she loved, she was in love with the Chief's nephew named Flying Eagle. Great Grandmother watched as the story of this young girl played out in her dream. The Chief's son walked over to the young Indian maid; he grabbed her arm and jerked her around facing him. He instructed her that she would belong to him, and there was nothing she could do to change that because her desires did not matter. She was unaware that when the Chief's son grabbed her arm and jerked her, the necklace fell to the ground. They argued; then the Indian maid ran back to the tent of her parents crying. She revealed to her parents what had occurred and how much she loved the Chief's nephew, her parents then asked for a council meeting with the Chief. Everyone involved including the Chief's brother and his son Flying Eagle spoke from their hearts. The nephew of the Chief (Flying Eagle) said how much he had always loved the maiden (Morning Dove) and how he desired to marry her. With the approval of the Chief, her parents, and the Chief's Brother (Flying Eagle's Dad) the wedding was planned and carried out. Morning-Dove was a beautiful bride, and the Indian ceremony was unique and beautiful, as well. Out of spite the Chief's son hid the necklace in a hollow of a tree, never would she wear this necklace again he said.

Great Grandmother had a peaceful feeling, as though a gentle, kind hearted, loving spirit was attached to this necklace that once belonged to the Indian Maiden. Great Grandmother awoke the next morning and told my Great Grandfather of her dream.

They both decided to donate this Indian artifact to the state museum with a description of my Great Grandmothers dream and when and where the necklace was acquired. DO YOU BELIEVE IT COULD

BE POSSIBLE FOR A SPIRIT TO BE ATTACHED TO AN ARTICIAL?

Chapter 9

Sonya's Story--Uncle Max and The Space Aliens

Uncle Max's story was told to only a few immediate family members by himself. Since everyone here is friends with my Uncle Max, I do not believe he would mind me telling you his incredible story.

In the summer of 1983 Uncle Max was leaving Florida with his 1975 Ford car, it was packed so full of his belongings he thought the doors would not close. He was beginning his journey to Texas in hopes of a promising new job. After driving for nearly nine hours with only food and bathroom breaks, he now was having difficulty staying awake. He yawned so much he decided to roll the driver side window down for some awakening fresh air, he then turned up the volume on the radio, but it did not help much. I need some toothpicks to pry my eyes open he thought as he looked at his wrist watch. It is one-fifteen in the morning, and I need to find a motel room somewhere so I can shower and get some much-needed sleep. How much worse can it get he thought, here I am on a remote road, and it may be some time before I can stop and get some sleep. I cannot find a lodging/motel available, and there is barely no traffic at this hour in the morning.

Are my eyes playing tricks on me, is that a vehicle light or is that something standing in the center of the road, these questions were running through his mind? As his car got a little closer, he recognized an unusual character that was wearing what appeared to be a silver jumpsuit. Within a couple of minutes Max felt a sharp, intense rays coming from the eyes of the figure on the road, this being was controlling his thoughts and actions. His car began to slow and then it came to a full stop. The driver side door of the car opened by itself and Max was willed to step out.

Max was visualizing what appears to be a space alien, he remembered seeing a random picture of what some people had described, but he never believed in any such thing. The alien was controlling Max's body and his thought process; the alien's eyes glowed with greenish yellow rays as it gave him orders to follow him. Max noticed how the alien never spoke with its mouth, just its eyes sent messages. For a total of two days, time-stood-still without any knowledge of the existence or presence of time.

Max started coming back to a standard realization as he found himself sitting upright under the steering wheel of his car. Max turned his head from side to side to look for any signs to tell him where he was. His car was sitting in a parking space close to a local motel office building. When Max assumed he was stable enough to stand, he went to the motel office to rent a room. Afterward, he returned to his car to get a changing of clothes, toothbrush, and toothpaste from his luggage. The room rental ticket told him he was in Texas, and by the date written on the ticket three full days had passed since he first left the state of Florida. How did I get here and where have I been for the last two days he thought? After opening the phone book in search of a nearby pizza delivery place, he called and ordered a pizza and a drink.

Then Max took a much-needed shower. After a good hot shower, Max began to feel like his self again but for some unknown reason there was a multitude of small to medium size bruises and puncture sites all over his body. Just after Max turned on the television, he sat down to relax. Within a couple of minutes the pizza delivery guy was knocking at the door of the motel room, Max paid him for the pizza and soft drink. Max did not realize just how hungry and thirsty he was, but he devoured all of that small pizza and a cold soft drink.

Max positioned two pillows to his head and back as he watched television while lying on his bed. Max picked up the remote control to scan for something interesting on television. The reporter of the local news in that vicinity spoke the word spaceship, and it caught Max's attention. The reporter told of numerous unidentified flying objects that had been seen in three different states, and several people had also reported that aliens had abducted them. The news reporter person told how a follow up would be made after test were completed for the public who believed they were abducted.   Could that have happened to me?   That would explain a lot, Max mysteriously thought to himself.   Before long Max drifted off to sleep with the television still playing.

While Max was asleep, his mind was processing itself, as if it were a computer that had just rebooted up.   Max began to visualize all of the events that had occurred to him since his car pulled out of the driveway at his rented apartment in Florida. He remembered driving his car when he saw a figure standing in the road, he also remembers following the Alien and going into what appeared to be a spacecraft. Once in that spacecraft he was levitated in a supine position, without a table beneath him. Three space beings were using weird instruments on his head as well as his body. Sometimes they would even point with one of their three digits and a beam of light would reflect somewhere in or on his body. The beings were all silver in color except for their eyes that glowed greenish yellow. One of the very last things Max remembered while he was in that spacecraft was a being that looked like it could have been his twin brother, but I never had a twin he thought to himself. Max said the being walked up to one of the Aliens standing near him, and he looked just like a mirrored image of himself. He told how he believed they took some of his cells to create a clone and once they were done, they released him. The next thing Max remembered was waking up and finding himself sitting in his car near the motel rental office. Max relived every event in his dream that night. When he woke up the next morning, Max was certain Aliens had abducted and cloned him. Max never reported this incident to the police but eventually he told his immediate family members.

Max went for that job interview, and he was delighted he got it. Max has a happy life, he is married and they have two children. On occasion, Max wonders about the Aliens and the clone of himself. He is curious about the reason for his abduction and from where in the universe they call home.

Chapter 10

Lora's Story (My Story)--Revenge at the Haunted Grover Mansion

I am going to tell you the story that my Aunt Gail previously disclosed to me, it occurred when she was in her junior year of high school.

Aunt Gail and her very best friend named Jane were both juniors that year in school. Gail and Jane were supposed to have a double date with seniors called Mike and Brad last Saturday night, but after waiting impatiently for two hours the boys never showed. They had planned to go out to eat and to dance at the famous local hangout that most teenagers in their circle of friends often visit.

The girls were so angry for being stood

up, they decided they were not going to wait by the phone for Mike and Brad any longer. They left home and went straight to the local hangout, Gail and Jane thought that maybe they could find out why they had been stood up. Once they arrived at their favorite meeting place, they spotted Brad and Mike sitting at a corner table with two unknown girls that appeared to be much younger, maybe in the eighth or ninth grade of school. Gail and Jane ordered sandwiches, fries, and drinks after they found a table as far away from Mike, and Brad as they could find. The girls decided they would both brush them off if they come up to their table to chat. Within a few minutes Gail and Jane started laughing uncontrollably about how Mike and Brad could stand them up for a couple of kids, everyone turned and looked their way.

Curiosity was killing the guys, what would these girls have to laugh about, after being stood up they thought? Brad and Mike each approached Jane and Gail's table. The guys made up some lame excuse that Brad's car had to be taken to a garage to be repaired before they could pick them up for their date. The girls replied, "Are you guys telling us that the garage did not have a telephone?" Both Mike and Brad's faces turned crimson-red. Next the girls made a comment about the boys robbing the cradle. Jane laughed and said, "You guys better go on back to the kids your babysitting!" The boys dropped their heads as they turned to leave, thinking to themselves, we will never...ever...stand a chance with Gail or Jane again.

On Monday at school the word had already spread like wildfire that Gail and

Brad, Jane and Mike had broken up, most everyone already knew what had occurred. The girls debated the situation, they decided the only way they would ever consider dating those boys again, would be if they could teach them a lesson. The girls spread the word around school that on Halloween night, which happens to be on a full moon this year, they are going to host a Haunted Masquerade Ball at the Old Grover Mansion. Everyone will be required to wear a costume and mask while at the Masquerade Ball. Halloween, that year would be the following Saturday of that week, and the Masquerade Ball would last from eight that night until two o'clock in the morning. The Grover Mansion stands approximately two miles from school, it is over one hundred and ten years old. Thomas Grover II willed it to his son Thomas

Grover III. Over sixty years ago Thomas Grover III, his wife Mary and their five-year-old daughter Annie died in an accident. One of the wheels on their carriage broke while they were out for a ride. The horses got spooked; this triggered them to run frantically as the carriage rolled over and thrashed about, causing the family to be thrown to their death.

People around the state believe the mansion is very haunted. Spirit mediums have done séances, and ghost hunters have visited the estate, they all left with a real belief in some spirits being present. It has also been reported that ghostly figures have been seen walking by windows as they carry lit candles. One group of ghost hunters recorded a young child giggling as they heard what sounded like a ball being bounced in the corridor, they felt high-energy activity present, or so they said.

Everyone in the junior and senior class at school except Mike and Brad is aware that when the clock strikes eleven-forty a séance will be taking place in the room near the coffin. The girls thought a séance would make the haunting seem real since it was going to be a Haunted Halloween Masquerade Ball. Gail and Jane will lock the doors at this time so no one can escape. Then, at eleven forty-five Dracula will rise from the coffin with a sword by his side. That sword will appear to have blood on it, and he will be searching for Brad and Mike. Gail and Jane will be helping Dracula find the guys with an avengement of their own for standing them up. We will forgive Brad and Mike only after they promise never to break another date with us again. The rooms will remain dusty, and the real cobwebs will not be disturbed. The only lights will be with lit candles and a couple of candelabras that belonged to the Grover family. The kitchen area of the mansion will be lit with candles, and the drinks will be in coolers' with ice except for a punch bowl that will be sitting at a table with cups nearby. Finger sandwiches, chips, and peanuts will be spread out for snacks on the table also. A portable battery operated radio will be playing until eleven-thirty, and then the night will get more exciting from the haunting of the séance and Dracula.

Saturday the girls and Jane's Uncle Allen, who is going to play the part of Dracula, decorated the mansion for the Masquerade Ball. The coffin is in place, and near the coffin a round table with chairs has been put for the séance to occur. He has painted some areas of the sword blade red to look as if blood has been shed with this sword. Allen's costume and the mask are ready to slip on.

The real cobwebs and dust makes everything look creepy. The matches are available to light the candles when the time is right. The radio is in place with the antenna up for the best possible reception. All of the shutters hang freely on the windows of the mansion and when the wind blows they make a creaking, slamming sound.

The girls left to go home at six-thirty to get dressed, both of them will be dressing as female vampires. Gail and Jane will use plastic fangs that have small particles that appear to look like blood on the attached teeth. They will also wear half face mask so the vampire teeth will show. By seven-forty in the evening, they have arrived back at the mansion: Gail, Jane, and Jane's Uncle Allen are already dressed. Allen takes his place in the coffin and tries to get comfortable for the long wait. "It is good that Allen does not have claustrophobia," Jane said. Gail nods her head in agreement.

At seven-fifty-five, most everyone has arrived all dressed in their costumes with their mask on, to suit the Haunting Halloween Season. The two of them light the candelabras, and then they light the candles that are in the rooms on the first and second floors of the Grover Mansion. Everything seems to be in place, and most everyone is already there.

Gail and Jane recognized Mike and Brad's voices when they were overheard talking to each other. Mike is dressed as a werewolf and Brad is dressed as a prisoner with a ball and chain attached to his ankles.   The Masquerade Halloween Ball is a blast, and everyone seems to be talking and enjoying themselves.   The old wind up clock shows it is eleven-forty at night.   Gail and Jane locked each of the doors that lead out of the mansion.   The people that agreed to do the séance is beginning to start, they chant and sway in their chairs.   Things are incredibly spooky looking; the séance draws everyone attention including Mike and Brad.

All of a sudden out of nowhere the shutters covering the windows slam open then closed and open again, and the candles flicker.   This sudden fright makes the hair stand up on everyone's arms.   "That was so creepy, we did not plan that," Jane said. The séance is still underway as the coffin lid rises up, and Dracula slowly sit's upward in the wooden box.   Dracula holds up the stained red blood appearing sword as he waves it back and forth. Dracula says, "Who Are Two That Stood Them Up-- REPENT I SAY!" Dracula exits the coffin, and the two lady vampires (Gail and Jane) join him. The three of them look right at Brad and Mike. Gail and Jane open their mouths slightly to reveal their fangs, and they say, "Revenge is ours, you stood us up." Mike and Brad makes a run for the front door, but it is locked, and Brad is slowed down by the ball and chain on his ankles. Mike tries to help Brad escape, but Jane, Gail, and Dracula grabs the two of them by the neck of their costume. Brad and Mike each kneel down, and they begin pleading for the girls to forgive them in front of their classmates. The boys promise never to stand them up on a date again. As the boys stand upright, the girls give them both a hug, and they tell them that they are forgiven.

However, not all was well, the séance was still in progress. Three of their classmates that were sitting in the chairs around that table were talking with the voices of the three dead owners of the estate. One had the voice of Thomas Grover III, the second voice was of Mary his wife and a third voice was Annie, their daughter. Thomas was upset that his home was being invaded. The two candelabras started floating in midair, and all of the locked doors flung open. Thomas Grover III demanded everyone to GET OUT NOW! An enormous puff of wind churned about causing the candles to blow out and the shutters to flap open and closed, back and forth. It is so dark, everyone is screaming and stumbling over each other trying to get out.　No one cares or gives any thought to the articles left behind.　Just as soon as everyone is out of the mansion the doors slam shut, and they lock tight.　As several of their classmates turn to look back toward the building, they see the shutters close tight over the windows.

Gail and Jane both remarked that the Grover family could keep anything that they had carried for the party, it was diffidently not worth them going back where they were not welcome.

I WOULD NOT GO BACK EITHER WOULD YOU?

Chapter 11

Is It The End OR Just The Beginning OF A New Camping Adventure?

It is now eleven-forty-five at night, and all of the stories have been told, we each have that burnt wood smell in our clothes. Most of us agree it is time for a bathroom break then we need some restful sleep. I am so sleepy, I can barely keep my eyes open as I enter the tent. I see that my friends are already getting comfortable in their sleeping bags, and I am more than ready to do the same.

Feeling safe and secure in our tent, we begin to talk about all of the stories we have heard tonight, we discuss which ones we believe to be true. All of a sudden we hear several owls hooting back and forth to each other as though they are caring on a conversation. Next we hear sounds like someone or something is scratching on the back of our shelter possibly using a small limb. "What is going on," Sonya said? I bet I know who is doing that, it has to be one of my naughty uncles playing a trick on us. This comment seems to calm my friends and soon we all get silent and drift off to sleep.

Bright and early the next morning (which is Saturday) we awaken to the delightful smell of bacon, sausage, and eggs. I crawl out of my sleeping bag, and I peek out of the camp door. I see mom cooking over a campfire, and I smell the aroma of coffee that is brewing. My friends are now getting up and out from their sleeping arrangements as the smell of the food circulates our tent. We stretch our arms and rub our eyes, and then each of us takes turns going to the bathroom in the woods, this is where we also change into some clean clothes. Our morning ritual is brushing our teeth and washing our face with some comforts of home, thanks to mom for bringing them along. By that time, mom is calling everyone to come and eat breakfast before it gets cold. After we finish eating everyone is more than ready to put in a full day of fishing.

We all board the boats and after we drift for a short time the boat motors are cranked, and then we head down the river to some of our family's favorite fishing spots. After fishing a little while, Bill says, "Fishing is much more fun than sitting at home being bored all day." Everyone agrees with Greg. The day is filled with amusement because we each have our episodes of underwater hangs and we keep getting our fishing lines hung in the overhead trees branches, as we cast our gears. We fish all day, and when we get hungry or thirsty, we have plenty of soft drinks, water, crackers and can food to keep us happy. With nine people fishing we have just about filled the coolers that we brought along with us, it is a good thing that the coolers are half filled with ice to keep the fish from spoiling.

After putting in a full day of fishing, we arrive back at the campsite. We got sunburnt, both from the sun glaring down on us and from the reflection of the sun bouncing back from the water. Fishing is fun, but I am exhausted. I believe everyone here would like to lay down and take a good nap, but we will have to wait until tonight.

After Seth cleans some of the fish, Uncle,

Doug and Uncle Kyle cooks them, to give mom and dad a break since mom has done most of the previous cooking. We eat so much that we become overstuffed and miserable.

Seth stands up not saying a word as he walks into the woods, maybe he went for a bathroom break, I think to myself. Within ten minutes Seth steps out from the trees as he swats at a couple of angry bees, clutched in his left arm he is holding a beehive dripping with fresh honey. He huffs and puffs as he gasps for breath, then he says, "Those bees were right on my heels, I do not think I have ever run so fast in all my life." Seth sits down and takes out his pocket knife, he is still clutching onto the beehive. After he catches his breath he cuts each of us a portion of the honeycomb, it is dripping with sweet raw honey. Dad says, "We even get dessert tonight, what is any better than nature's candy?" Different comments were being made from each of us: Gosh! Holly-Cow! Delicious! Great Day, This Is Good! We laugh at each other, as we observe the sticky sweet honey dripping from our chins.

Mom continuously yawns, so she and dad decides to call it a night. Seth also states the fact of being tired, he tells everyone good night as he is getting up to go to the same tent that my uncles share with him, to get some sleep. Uncle Doug reminds us that sometime tomorrow we will be returning home, this makes us unhappy to think our camping trip is almost over. We talk about the fun that we have had and how much we enjoyed the campfire stories. My friends and I yawn so much that we decide if we do not go to bed; we are going to fall asleep right here around the campfire.

Uncle Kyle and Uncle Doug stay up long after everyone else has ventured off to bed. Around two o'clock in the morning, my friends and I were awakened by something grunting and growling as it kept slapping at our tent. My friends and I begin yelling and screaming for help. At the same time, Uncle Kyle runs in and screams, "There is a bear right behind this tent, you need to get out now!" Dad heard us screaming, he grabbed his shotgun and ran out of his tent. In a panic, Seth runs out of the tent he was sleeping in to find out what is going on. Dad points his gun and starts to open fire on the bear. Uncle Kyle frantically runs to dad yelling, "Stop, Stop" as he tries to take the weapon from dad's hands, but it fires just over the bear's head! Kyle said, "Wait, that's Doug dressed up like a bear. Doug and I just wanted to scare the teenagers with this bear skin rug that we brought from his home." Dad said, "What in the world do you both mean, do you not know I could have killed my own brother, because of a foolish prank?"

I am not sure who ended up getting scared more. Will this incident teach Uncle Doug and Uncle Kyle a lesson about pulling pranks on others? Yikes, I think to myself, how quickly Uncle Doug's life could have ended right here. After everyone's nerves begin to calm down except for dads we return to our tents to try and get some much-needed sleep.

The next morning mom says, "Dad tossed and turned all night long." Dad is still upset with his brothers because he came so close to shooting Uncle Doug. At eight-thirty, this morning during breakfast, Uncle Doug, and Uncle Kyle apologize to everyone for the fake bear prank they pulled last night. Dad said, "If you guys ever decide to pull another prank, I suggest you let me in on it!" Uncle Doug and Uncle Kyle strongly agree that they should have informed dad of their plans.

By nine-fifteen this morning Dad's anger begins to subside with his brothers. Deep down my father knew they meant no harm, and that they were just trying to have a little playful fun, but that fun could have been very dangerous.

No one seems to be in a hurry to go home, so Uncle Doug, Dad and my friend Greg decide to do some more fishing.

I am craving something sweet so I ask mom if we can roast the other bag of marshmallows. I find them stored in a cooler with some other cooking supplies. Beth, Sonya, and I go in search of six new sticks, so each of us can have one to roast our own marshmallows on. Mom, Beth, Sonya, Seth, Uncle Kyle and I eat all of the toasty, gooey, yummy marshmallows, that's what it took to satisfy my sweet tooth.

Seth tells us that he knows where a natural piped well flows that has the best tasting cold water he has ever drunk. He says it flows so freely that no electrical pump is needed, and it is only a short walking distance from here. I can almost imagine tasting that fresh cold water, and I wonder if anyone else can picture that in his or her mind too. I ask Seth if he would show us where the well is, and he agrees to go. Now making our way, we walk through a slightly damp area. This area has different sizes and shapes of ferns and a few

Venus flytraps scattered about, we try to be extremely careful walking so we will not damage them. We walk about fifteen minutes before we can hear the free flowing water pouring from a pipe in the distance. Just before we approach the well, we walk close up to a doe and fawn drinking some of the water on the ground when they spot us they run away. Just a few more steps and we began drinking some of the water from this overflowing pipe. The water is so cold and refreshing, it is the best tasting water I have ever drunk as it gushes out of the tube. This pipe is almost ice-cold to the touch, it was once a natural small free flowing well until someone had an idea to put down that pipe. The continuous running water has cut a trench-like-stream in the ground. There is some lush dark emerald green vegetation that grows along the side of the stream. "What a lovely place to see," Mom says. When we left the camp to go visit this natural-spring-well mom brought an empty pitcher with her so Greg, Dad, and Uncle Doug could have some fresh water to drink when they return from fishing. Everyone thanks Seth for showing us the well, then we head back to the campsite.

Once we arrive back at the camp, mom suggests we all start packing for the return trip home. It takes approximately an hour to take the tents down and to get everything packed up neatly. When Dad, Greg, and Uncle Doug return to the campsite, they display all of their fish they caught, they are as proud of them as if they had won a trophy. Mom tells them about the natural running well as they drink some of the water from the pitcher, they each make a good comment about the refreshing taste.

Dad says, "It's time to get the boats loaded with our supplies, we need to begin our journey back home." Each person helps pack all the supplies and camping gear in the vessels, and next we put our life jackets on. Everyone begins to take a seat in one of the boats except my friends and I we remain standing on the river bank. The four of us plead with my parents to bring us back camping, at least one more time before school starts back? My parents agree that they will try to if possible. I guess that is the best answer we can get from them at this point. So, we now board the boats for the ride back to our vehicles. Once we arrive back at the boat dock where the vehicles and trailers were left, the men load the boats back on the trailers. It takes us approximately fifteen minutes of travel time to get back home. As we remove the camping equipment from each vessel, we neatly pack everything back in our storage building. It will be much easier to locate the camping supplies when we get ready for our next trip.

The week after our camping trip, my friends and I are anxiously awaiting and hoping for the next adventure down Long Winding River. It would be exciting to hear some new campfire stories. Do you think we should invite my uncles? I sure do, it would not be the same without them.

www.ingramcontent.com/pod-product-compliance
Lightning Source LLC
Chambersburg PA
CBHW060514030426
42337CB00015B/1887